FROM THE CHINESE

From the Chinese

EDITED BY

R. C. TREVELYAN

THE LIBRARY
COLBY JUNIOR COLLEGE
NEW LONDON, N. H.

Oxford
AT THE CLARENDON PRESS
1945

PL
3277
.E3
T7

OXFORD UNIVERSITY PRESS
AMEN HOUSE, E.C. 4
London Edinburgh Glasgow New York
Toronto Melbourne Capetown Bombay
Calcutta Madras
HUMPHREY MILFORD
PUBLISHER TO THE UNIVERSITY

27050

PRINTED IN GREAT BRITAIN AT THE UNIVERSITY PRESS, OXFORD
BY JOHN JOHNSON, PRINTER TO THE UNIVERSITY

ACKNOWLEDGEMENT

THANKS are due to the translators and publishers of the following books for permission to reprint the poems indicated.

Harold Acton and Ch'en Shih-Hsiang, *Modern Chinese Poetry* (G. Duckworth & Co., Ltd., 1936), for Nos. 51–62; Florence Ayscough and Amy Lowell, *Fir-flower Tablets* (Houghton Mifflin Co., 1922), for Nos. 7, 10, 11, 14, 17, and 23–5; E. D. Edwards, *The Dragon Book* (Wm. Hodge & Co., 1938), for Nos. 48–9; H. A. Giles, *Chinese Poetry* (Bernard Quaritch, Ltd., 1898), for Nos. 9, 13, 19, 20, 29, 43–5, and 47; A. Waley, *Book of Songs* (Allen & Unwin, Ltd., 1937) for Nos. 1–3; A. Waley, *More Translations* (Allen & Unwin, Ltd., 1919), for Nos. 36–7, 39, and 41; A. Waley, *The Temple* (Allen & Unwin, Ltd., 1923), for Nos. 4–6 and 46; A. Waley, *170 Chinese Poems* (Constable & Co., Ltd., 1918), for Nos. 8, 28, 38, and 40.

Nos. 12, 15, 16, 18, 21, 22, 26, 27, 30, 31, 32, 33–5, and 42 are reprinted from *The Jade Mountain* by Witter Bynner, by permission of, and special arrangement with, Alfred A. Knopf, Inc. Copyright 1920, 1921, 1922, 1923, 1924, 1925, 1926, 1927, 1928, 1929 by Alfred A. Knopf, Inc.

CONTENTS

INTRODUCTION

The civilization of the Chinese is by many centuries older than ours. It reached its highest point during the darkest and most barbarous period of our Middle Ages. Not long ago we discovered that their sculpture and painting, though now decadent, have at times been as great as any in the history of art; and to-day we are beginning to make much the same discovery about their poetry. No doubt there is a great deal that is trivial and conventional in Chinese, just as there is in European, literature: but in some of the poems here translated we may recognize qualities that are seldom found except in great poetry, I mean directness, simplicity, and sincerity. In these respects, and also in the perfection of their art, the best Chinese poets are not inferior to the Greek and English, although their range of thought and subject-matter may be much more limited.

What is known as classical poetry was chiefly written during the T'ang and Sung dynasties, from A.D. 618 to 1278. But conscious literary poetry had begun a thousand years earlier, in the fourth century B.C., and had gone on developing, or, rather, narrowing itself, until the T'ang period, when it flowered in the exquisite, but often very conventional, poems of the classical school.

Among the poets of the T'ang dynasty the most important are Li Po (A.D. 701–62), Tu Fu (712–70), and Po Chü-i (772–846). Chinese critics and English translators differ a good deal in their estimates of these poets; but the specimens included in this book will allow the reader to judge for himself. Li Po's 'Bringing in the Wine' (p. 20) is a magnificent Bacchanalian rhapsody; and of his

'Hard Roads in Shu' (p. 22) Mr. Waley writes: 'With its wild profusion of long and short lines, its cataract of exotic verbiage, he aimed at something nearer akin to music than poetry.' Mr. Waley's own favourite is Po Chü-i. I have included a few of his delightful autobiographical poems, and Mr. Witter Bynner's fine versions of his two more ambitious poems, 'A Song of Unending Sorrow' and 'The Song of a Guitar'.

These classical poems imply a very high level of culture: in fact there have been few societies so refined as that of the Chinese educated class during this period. But this civilization had one defect, which it shared with the civilization of Athens at the time of Pericles. Women were generally treated as inferior beings to men, and were regarded as little more than domestic drudges and mothers of children. It will be noticed how frequent in these pages is the theme of friendship between men. The favourite theme of European poetry is love. But except in popular songs, or in the laments of deserted wives and mistresses, there has been almost no Chinese love-poetry, whereas friendship is a common subject, often very beautifully and poignantly treated.

I think it will be agreed that the poems here translated do not remind us of English poems of any period. It is in fact a great help to the imagination that these quite un-European poems should be presented to us in forms where both the rhythm and the diction are completely disinfected of anything that might suggest the conventions and artifices of English poetry. An exception, however, should be made of the late Professor Giles's rhymed translations, which are often felicitously Chinese in spirit, though English in form.

Chinese classical lyrics were frequently written in lines each consisting of five monosyllables. Mr. Waley has been successful in solving the problem of how to suggest this Chinese five-syllable metre in a language such as ours, which is by no means monosyllabic. He has used a line of five stresses, with unaccented syllables interposed between them. Here are the first two lines of the poem of Po Chü-i translated on page 88 of his *More Translations from the Chinese:*

Yü chün chü lao yeh:
Tzu wen, lao ho ju?

A literal translation of this would be:

With you together old become;
Self ask, age what like?

In Mr. Waley's translation these lines appear as:

We are growing old together, you and I.
Let us ask ourselves, what is old age like?

Here in each line there are various unstressed syllables between the five main stresses; yet I think that the essential structure and swing of the Chinese rhythm is adequately suggested in the translation, which at the same time makes a charming and natural English poem in accentual metre.

Another Chinese verse-form consists of lines, not of five, but of seven syllables, with a slight pause between the fourth and fifth stresses. The poem of Po Chü-i on page 80 of Mr. Waley's *More Translations* is a good example.

Here are the last four lines:

The dog lies curled on the stone steps, for the earth is wet with dew;
The birds come near to the window and chatter, telling that the day is fine.

With the lingering fumes of yesterday's wine my head is still heavy;
With new doffing of winter clothes my body has grown light.

And here we may notice a literary device very common in Chinese poetry, called parallelism. The phrasing of the second line of a couplet is often made to correspond very closely to the phrasing of the preceding line. If we read the two last lines of Po Chü-i's poem, omitting a few small connecting words which do not occur in the Chinese—

Lingering fumes yesterday wine head still heavy;
New doffing winter clothes body grown light—

we shall see how very close is the correspondence of word and phrase in the two lines. This artifice can be charming and effective, if used with discretion; but with later poets it sometimes degenerates into a tiresome mannerism.

Neither Mr. Witter Bynner nor Miss Lowell has attempted to reproduce the Chinese metrical pattern so closely as Mr. Waley. They have no doubt found more ease and freedom in their somewhat less rigid methods, which their many successes have fully justified.

Rhyme patterns of various kinds were used in all Chinese poetry; but translators have seldom attempted rhyme, 'because (to quote Mr. Waley) it is impossible to produce in English rhyme-effects at all similar to those of the original, where the same rhyme sometimes runs through a whole poem: also, because the restrictions of rhyme necessarily injure either the vigour of one's language or the literalness of one's version'.

There are, I think, certain characteristics common to most of these poems, which are not generally found in European, or indeed in other Oriental, poetry. To begin with, they are deliberately tranquil and sober in tone. There is no excitement about them, no ecstasy, little or no rhetoric: there are few adjectives, and very few metaphors or similes. They are usually composed of simple statements of fact or of sensations, artfully arranged so as to convey some idea or sentiment. They seldom aim at dramatic or narrative effect; yet they are often exceedingly human. Po Chü-i is not the only poet who, when he chooses, is the master of a quiet but very moving pathos. But he is exceptional in his power of interesting us in his own most attractive personality; and in this he might seem to have some affinity with such European writers as Horace and Montaigne.

One very delightful quality of Chinese poetry is its power of expressing a delicate and intimate feeling for the beauty of Nature, such as we find also in Chinese painting. Sometimes these nature-poems are pervaded by a gentle, rather sad mysticism, very different from the ardent, ecstatic raptures of Persian or Indian poetry. Taoism was a mystical philosophy which from very early times had a great influence on men of culture, especially on painters and poets. The Taoist ideal was to withdraw from the vanities of the world of affairs, and live in tranquil communion with Nature among forests and streams and hills. It appealed strongly to the more refined among the highly educated governing class. Thus it was a moral and aesthetic yearning to escape from worldliness, rather than a passionate desire for union with God, that was continually tempting these cultivated scholars and gentlemen to play truant from their official duties and retire to the mountains in search of contemplative solitude, to which they often gave exquisite expression in their paintings and poems.

Perhaps the most important historical reason for these undramatic and quietistic qualities of Chinese literature is that it did not originate in epic poetry, as did European literature. The *Iliad* and *Odyssey* within their narrative structures contain intensely dramatic elements. They are full not only of tragic action, but of vivid characters, dramatically contrasted. It was thus quite natural that Greek drama should grow out of Homer, and Greek lyrical poetry too, which always had a tendency to be dramatic in spirit, though not in form. Ever since then, this dramatic instinct has been the common inheritance of Western literature, whether narrative or lyrical. No Chinese poet could have written anything remotely resembling Milton's *Paradise Lost* or his *Hymn to the Nativity*, or Shelley's *Ode to the West Wind*.

On the other hand it would not be easy to find European parallels to Chinese poetry. Occasionally something of the same kind appears in German literature. There are poems of Goethe and Heine that might have been written by a Chinaman. Our own Hardy too has a Chinese side to him, though he is usually too dramatic and not exquisite enough. And here is a song of Shelley's that might almost have been composed in ninth-century China:

A widow bird sat mourning for her love
Upon a wintry bough;
The frozen wind crept on above,
The freezing stream below.

There was no leaf upon the forest bare,
No flower upon the ground,
And little motion in the air
Except the mill-wheel's sound.

Compare this with a poem by Li Po translated by Mr. Waley:

> The fields are chill; the sparse rain has stopped;
> The colours of Spring teem on every side.
> With leaping fish the blue pond is full;
> With singing thrushes the green boughs droop.
> The flowers of the field have dabbled their powdered
>   cheeks;
> The mountain grasses are bent level at the waist.
> By the bamboo stream the last fragment of cloud
> Blown by the wind slowly scatters away.

While this song is a piece of pure landscape poetry, the English song is emotionally dominated by its first line: 'A widow bird sat mourning for her love.' Though this is not human drama, but bird-drama, the tone is none the less dramatic as well as contemplative.

Such facts go a long way to account both for the limitations and for the peculiar excellences of Chinese classical literature. Poetry that is neither dramatic, passionate, nor rapturous, has no need to shape itself into large and elaborate designs. It can indulge instead in quiet subtleties and delicacies, for which our more energetic and rhetorical poetry has seldom the leisure. Rhetoric is the sum of the various artifices that are needed to sustain the movement of poems of large design. For the Chinese, who preferred to write short poems, and so could dispense with rhetoric, there was gain as well as loss. Their poetry is generally deficient in range and vitality and splendour: it is content with the charm of exquisiteness, intimacy, and sincerity.

A quality which poems on a small scale must possess, if they are to be works of art, is perfection of form. Faults of style and occasional lack of coherence may be overlooked or pardoned in a long poem; but in a short lyric, which takes a minute or so to read, perfection of form and phrase, and unity of mood are necessities; and here the best Chinese poets show themselves to be great masters. As to the physical beauty and verbal harmony of their poetry I have no right to speak; but I understand it to be true that quite as much artistic thought and labour have been devoted to such matters by the Chinese as by poets of any other race.

But in spite of all the marked differences between the Chinese classics and those of every other literature, whether Western or Eastern, in spite of the absence of epics, and, until the thirteenth century, of dramas, of love-poetry, and of rhetoric, yet if we go back to primitive times we shall find that poetry in its popular origins was not so very different to poetry in other countries. China, no less than Germany, Spain, Greece, and India, had (and indeed still has) her folk-songs and ballads. I have included (pages 1 and 2) two pieces of folk-song type from the *Book of Odes*, which are certainly earlier than 500 B.C. The few popular ballads that survive have a remarkable resemblance in style and subject-matter to the ballads of other peoples all the world over.

But poetry, though its origins in China were so similar to those of poetry everywhere else, did not, for whatever reasons, develop there upon the same lines as in other countries. Some of the more obvious reasons I have tried to suggest; but the fundamental causes probably lie deeper, in the economic and social structure of Far Eastern civilization, and in the racial character and imagination. Yet it is an interesting fact that the earliest consciously artistic poetry has far more resemblance to the poetry of other literatures than has the later classical verse. During the Han dynasty, between 206 B.C. and A.D. 220, when China was emerging from a feudal and semi-barbaric society into a more stable and cultured civilization, a number of poems were written, which in style and subject-matter were very different from the classical types. They were composed, not in symmetrical stanzas, but in irregular verses of changing character. Some of these poems are of considerable length; and they often show a vigour and breadth of imagination unlike anything else in Chinese literature. 'The Bones of Chuang Tzu' is a poem that need not fear comparison with Lucretius and Leopardi at their greatest; and 'The Wangsun' is a delightful and perfectly composed masterpiece.

It is evident that Chinese poetry had changed very considerably during the long journey of a thousand years which it travelled between the primitive grandeur and imaginative energy of such poems, and the quiet charm and delicacy of Po Chü-i and the classical writers. Perhaps one of the reasons for this change was that poetry, which was at first a rare and somewhat aristocratic accomplishment, gradually became an almost national habit. In the competitive examinations, which until a few years ago were the only entrance to a public career, the ability to compose a respectable set of verses upon given themes was one of the most important qualifications. Most men of education, and many women too, were competent and habitual versifiers, though no doubt very few were real poets. The result of this would inevitably be that, while skill in writing verse according to the traditional rules would become widely diffused, originality and true poetic imagination would be less and less appreciated, and in time would die out. This is what in fact happened. But in the eighth and ninth centuries a great deal of genuine poetry was still being written: and even after vital creative power seemed for the time to have almost faded out of the art of poetry, there survived a loving knowledge and admiration of the great classical writers, and of those greater primitive poets of two thousand years ago.

There are several specialized kinds of poetry which are not represented in this book, particularly the tz'ŭ, a lyrical form in unequal lines, in metres derived from musical melodies. This was a favourite form in the Sung dynasty and for some time afterwards. The actual words used are so much more important than the content of this kind of poetry, that it presents peculiar difficulties to the translator, and no satisfactory tz'ŭ in English are available. The best in any European language are the very free versions of Judith Gautier in her *Livre de Jade*.

The twelve modern poems at the end of this book, that are so admirably translated by Harold Acton and Ch'en Shih-Hsiang, give clear evidence that poetry in China is once more not only very much alive, but is endeavouring with some success to solve various new problems presented by a rapidly changing world, and by a language that is continually altering and growing. However experimental both in form and subject-matter these young writers may be (they are all of them born within the present century), they show no sign of having forgotten or renounced the heritage that has come down to them from the great writers of the past.

ANONYMOUS

1

The Broken Faith

If along the highroad
I caught hold of your sleeve,
Do not hate me;
Old ways take time to overcome.

If along the highroad
I caught hold of your hand
Do not be angry with me;
Friendship takes time to overcome.

ARTHUR WALEY

2

Agricultural Song

Who says you have no sheep?
Three hundred is the flock.
Who says you have no cattle?
Ninety are the black-lips.
Here your rams come,
Their horns thronging;
Here your cattle come,
Their ears flapping.

ANONYMOUS

Some go down the slope,
Some are drinking in the pool,
Some are sleeping, some waking.
Here your herdsmen come
In rush-cloak and bamboo-hat,
Some shouldering their dinners.
Only thirty brindled beasts!
Your sacrifices will not go short.

Your herdsman comes,
Bringing faggots, bringing brushwood,
With cock-game, with hen-game.
Your rams come,
Sturdy and sound;
None that limps, none that ails.
He beckons to them with raised arm;
All go up into the stall.

Your herdsman dreams,
Dreams of locusts and fish,
Of banners and flags.
A wise man explains the dreams:
'Locusts and fishes
Mean fat years.
Flags and banners
Mean a teeming house and home.'

ARTHUR WALEY

3

Dynastic Song

So they appeared before their lord the king
To get from him their emblems,
Dragon-banners blazing bright,
Tuneful bells tinkling,
Bronze-knobbed reins jangling—
The gifts shone with glorious light.
Then they showed them to their shining ancestors
Piously, making offering,
That they might be vouchsafed long life,
Everlastingly be guarded.
O, a mighty store of blessings!
Glorious and mighty, those former princes and lords
Who secure us with many blessings,
Through whose bright splendours
We greatly prosper.

ARTHUR WALEY

CHANG HÊNG (A.D. 78–139)

4

The Bones of Chuang Tzu

I, CHANG P'ING-TZU, had traversed the Nine Wilds and
seen their wonders,
In the eight continents beheld the ways of Man,
The Sun's procession, and the orbit of the Stars,

The surging of the dragon, the soaring of the Phoenix
in his flight.
In the red desert to the south I sweltered,
And northward waded through the wintry burghs of Yu.
Through the Valley of Darkness to the west I wandered,
And eastward travelled to the Sun's extreme abode,
The stooping Mulberry Tree.

So the seasons sped; weak autumn languished,
A small wind woke the cold.

And now with rearing of rein-horse,
Plunging of the tracer, round I fetched
My high-roofed chariot to westward.
Along the dykes we loitered, past many meadows,
And far away among the dunes and hills.
Suddenly I looked and by the road-side
I saw a man's bones lying in the squelchy earth,
Black rime-frost over him; and I in sorrow spoke
And asked him, saying, 'Dead man, how was it?
Fled you with your friend from famine and for the last
grains
Gambled and lost? Was this earth your tomb,
Or did floods carry you from afar? Were you mighty,
were you wise,
Were you foolish and poor? A warrior or a girl?'
Then came a wonder; for out of the silence a voice—
Thin echo only, in no substance was the spirit seen—
Mysteriously answered, saying, 'I was a man of Sung,
Of the clan of Chuang; Chou was my name.
Beyond the climes of common thought

My reason soared, yet could I not save myself;
For at the last, when the long charter of my years was told,
I too, for all my magic, by Age was brought
To the Black Hill of Death.
Wherefore, O Master, do you question me?'
Then I answered:
'Let me plead for you upon the Five Hill-tops,
Let me pray for you to the Gods of Heaven and the Gods
 of Earth,
That your white bones may arise,
And your limbs be joined anew.
The God of the North shall give me back your ears;
I will scour the Southland for your eyes;
From the sunrise will I wrest your feet;
The West shall yield your heart.
I will set each several organ in its throne;
Each subtle sense will I restore.
Would you not have it so?'
The dead man answered me:
'O Friend, how strange and unacceptable your words!
In death I rest and am at peace; in life I toiled and strove.
Is the hardness of the winter stream
Better than the melting of spring?
All the pride that the body knew,
Was it not lighter than dust?
What Chʻao and Hsü despised,
What Po-chʻêng fled,
Shall I desire, whom death
Already has hidden in the Eternal Way—
Where Li Chu cannot see me,

Nor Tzu Yeh hear me,
Where neither Yao nor Shun can praise me,
Nor wolf nor tiger harm me,
Lance prick me nor sword wound me?
Of the Primal Spirit is my substance; I am a wave
In the river of Darkness and Light.
The Maker of All Things is my Father and Mother,
Heaven is my bed and earth my cushion,
The thunder and lightning are my drum and fan,
The sun and moon my candle and my torch,
The Milky Way my moat, the stars my jewels.
With nature am I conjoined;
I have no passion, no desire.
Wash me and I shall be no whiter,
Foul me and I shall yet be clean.
I come not, yet am here;
Hasten not, yet am swift.'
The voice stopped, there was silence.
A ghostly light
Faded and expired.
I gazed upon the dead, stared in sorrow and compassion.
Then I called upon my servant that was with me
To tie his silken scarf about those bones
And wrap them in a cloak of sombre dust;
While I, as offering to the soul of this dead man,
Poured my hot tears upon the margin of the road.

ARTHUR WALEY

5

The Dancers of Huai-nan

(A FRAGMENT)

I saw them dancing at Huai-nan and made this poem of praise:

THE instruments of music are made ready,
Strong wine is in our cups;
Flute-songs flutter and a din of magic drums.
Sound scatters like foam, surges free as a flood . . .
And now when the drinkers were all drunken,
And the sun had fallen to the west,
Up rose the fair ones to the dance,
Well painted and apparelled,
In veils of soft gossamer
All wound and meshed;
And ribbons they unravelled,
And scarfs to bind about their heads.
The wielder of the little stick
Whispers them to their places, and the steady drums
Draw them through the mazes of the dance.
They have raised their long sleeves, they have covered their eyes;
Slowly their shrill voices
Swell the steady song.
And the song said:
As a frightened bird whose love
Has wandered away from the nest,
I flutter my desolate wings.

For the wind blows back to my home,
And I long for my father's house.

Subtly from slender hips they swing,
Swaying, slanting delicately up and down.
And like the crimson mallow's flower
Glows their beauty, shedding flames afar.
They lift languid glances,
Peep distrustfully, till of a sudden
Ablaze with liquid light
Their soft eyes kindle. So dance to dance
Endlessly they weave, break off and dance again.
Now flutter their cuffs like a great bird in flight,
Now toss their white sleeves like whirling snow.
So the hours go by, till now at last
The powder has blown from their cheeks, the black from
their brows,
Flustered now are the fair faces, pins of pearl
Torn away, tangled the black tresses.
With combs they catch and gather in
The straying locks, put on the gossamer gown
That trailing winds about them, and in unison
Of body, song and dress, obedient
Each shadows each, as they glide softly to and fro.

ARTHUR WALEY

WANG YEN-SHOU (*circa* A.D. 130)

6

The Wangsun

SUBLIME was he, stupendous of invention,
Who planned the miracles of earth and sky.
Wondrous the power that charged
Small things with secret beauty, moving in them all.
See now the wangsun, crafty creature, mean of size,
Uncouth of form; the wrinkled face
Of an aged man; the body of a little child.
See how in turn he blinks and blenches with an air
Pathetically puzzled, dimly gazes
Under tired lids, through languid lashes
Looks tragic and hollow-eyed, rumples his brow,
Scatters this way and that
An insolent, astonished glare;
Sniffs and snorts, snuffs and sneezes,
Snicks and cocks his knowing little ears!
Now like a dotard mouths and chews;
Or hoots and hisses through his pouted lips;
Shows gnashing teeth, grates and grinds ill-temperedly,
Gobbles and puffs and scolds.
And every now and then,
Down to his belly, from the larder that he keeps
In either cheek, he sends
Little consignments lowered cautiously.
Sometimes he squats
Like a puppy on its haunches, or hare-like humps
An arching back;

Smirks and wheedles with ingratiating sweetness;
Or suddenly takes to whining, surly snarling;
Then, like a ravening tiger, roars.

He lives in thick forests, deep among the hills,
Or houses in the clefts of sharp precipitous rocks.
Alert and agile is his nature, nimble are his wits;
Swift are his contortions,
Apt to every need,
Whether he climb tall tree-stems of a hundred feet,
Or sways on the shuddering shoulder of a long bough.
Before him, the dark gullies of unfathomable streams;
Behind, the silent hollows of the lonely hills.
Twigs and tendrils are his rocking-chairs,
On rungs of rotting wood he trips
Up perilous places; sometimes leap after leap,
Like lightning flits through woods.
Sometimes he saunters with a sad, forsaken air;
Then suddenly peeps round,
Beaming with satisfaction. Up he springs,
Leaps and prances, whoops, and scampers on his way.
Up cliffs he scrambles, up pointed rocks,
Dances on shale that shifts or twigs that snap,
Suddenly swerves and lightly passes. . . .
Oh, what tongue could unravel
The tale of all his tricks?

Alas, one trait
With the human tribe he shares; their sweet 's his sweet,
Their bitter is his bitter. Off sugar from the vat

Or brewers' dregs he loves to sup.
So men put wine where he will pass.
How he races to the bowl,
How nimbly licks and swills!
Now he staggers, feels dazed and foolish,
Darkness falls upon his eyes. . . .
He sleeps and knows no more.
Up steal the trappers, catch him by the mane,
Then to a string or ribbon tie him, lead him home;
Tether him in the stable or lock him into the yard;
Where faces all day long
Gaze, gape, gasp at him and will not go away.

ARTHUR WALEY

T'AO CH'IEN (A.D. 365–427)

7

Once more Fields and Gardens

EVEN as a young man
I was out of tune with ordinary pleasures.
It was my nature to love the rooted hills,
The high hills which look upon the four edges of Heaven.
What folly to spend one's life like a dropped leaf
Snared under the dust of streets!
But for thirteen years it was so I lived.

The caged bird longs for the fluttering of high leaves.
The fish in the garden pool languishes for the whirled water
Of meeting streams.

T'AO CH'IEN

So I desired to clear and seed a patch of the wild Southern
moor.
And always a countryman at heart,
I have come back to the square enclosures of my fields
And to my walled garden with its quiet paths.

Mine is a little property of ten *mou* or so,
A thatched house of eight or nine rooms.
On the North side the eaves are overhung
With the thick leaves of elm-trees,
And willow-trees break the strong force of the wind.
On the South, in front of the great hall,
Peach-trees and plum-trees spread a net of branches
Before the distant view.

The village is hazy, hazy,
And mist sucks over the open moor.
A dog barks in the sunken lane which runs through the
village.
A cock crows, perched on a clipped mulberry.

There is no dust or clatter
In the courtyard before my house.
My private rooms are quiet,
And calm with the leisure of moonlight through an open
door.

For a long time I have lived in a cage;
Now I have returned.
For one must return
To fulfil one's nature.

AMY LOWELL

8

New Corn

SWIFTLY the years, beyond recall.
Solemn the stillness of this fair morning.
I will clothe myself in spring-clothing
And visit the slopes of the Eastern Hill.
By the mountain-stream a mist hovers,
Hovers a moment, then scatters.
There comes a wind blowing from the south
That brushes the fields of new corn.

ARTHUR WALEY

CH'ÊN TZŬ-ANG (A.D. 656–98)

9

Regrets

MY eyes saw not the men of old;
And now their age away has rolled
I weep—to think I shall not see
The heroes of posterity.

H. A. GILES

WANG WEI (A.D. 699–759)

10

The Blue-green Stream

EVERY time I have started for the Yellow Flower River,
I have gone down the Blue-Green Stream,
Following the hills, making ten thousand turnings.
We go along rapidly, but advance scarcely one hundred *li*.
We are in the midst of a noise of water,
Of the confused and mingled sounds of water broken by
stones,
And in the deep darkness of pine-trees.
Rocked, rocked,
Moving on and on,
We float past water-chestnuts
Into a clearness reflecting reeds and rushes.
My heart is clean and white as silk; it has already achieved
Peace;
It is smooth as the placid river.
I long to stay here, curled up on the rocks,
Dropping my fish-line for ever.

AMY LOWELL

11

Farm-house on the Wei Stream

THE slanting sun shines on the cluster of small houses
upon the heights.
Oxen and sheep are coming home along the distant lane.
An old countryman is thinking of the herd-boy,
He leans on his staff by the thorn-branch gate, watching.
Pheasants are calling, the wheat is coming into ear,
Silk-worms sleep, the mulberry-leaves are thin.
Labourers, with their hoes over their shoulders, arrive;
They speak pleasantly together, loth to part.
It is for this I long—unambitious peace!
Disappointed in my hopes, dissatisfied, I hum 'Dwindled
and Shrunken'.

AMY LOWELL

12

My Retreat at Mount Chung-nan

MY heart in middle age found the Way,
And I came to dwell at the foot of this mountain.
When the spirit moves, I wander alone
Amid beauty that is all for me. . . .
I will walk till the water checks my path,
Then sit and watch the rising clouds—
And some day meet an old wood-cutter
And talk and laugh and never return.

WITTER BYNNER

13

A Rencontre

Sir, from my dear home you come,
And all its glories you can name;
Oh tell me—has the winter-plum
Yet blossomed o'er the window-frame?

H. A. GILES

NIU HSI-CHI (*circa* A.D. 730)

14

Sung to the Tune of 'The Unripe Hawthorn Berry'

Mist is trying to hide the Spring-coloured hills,
The sky is pale, the stars are scattered and few.
The moon is broken and fading, yet there is light on your face,
These are the tears of separation, for now it is bright dawn.

We have said many words,
But our passion is not assuaged.
Turn your head, I have still something to say:
Remember my skirt of green open-work silk,
The sweet-scented grasses everywhere will prevent your forgetting.

AMY LOWELL

CH'ANG CHIEN (8TH CENTURY)

15

At Wang Ch'ang-Ling's Retreat

HERE, beside a clear deep lake,
You live accompanied by clouds;
Or soft through the pine the moon arrives
To be your own pure-hearted friend.
You rest under thatch in the shadow of your flowers,
Your dewy herbs flourish in their bed of moss.
Let me leave the world. Let me alight, like you,
On your western mountain with phoenixes and cranes.

WITTER BYNNER

LI YI (8TH CENTURY)

16

On hearing a Flute at Night from the Wall of Shou-Hsiang

THE sand below the border-mountain lies like snow,
And the moon like frost beyond the city-wall,
And someone somewhere, playing a flute,
Has made the soldiers homesick all night long.

WITTER BYNNER

LI PO (A.D. 701–62)

17

A Farewell Banquet to My Father's Younger Brother Yün, the Imperial Librarian

WHEN I was young, I spent the white days lavishly.
I sang—I laughed—I boasted of my ruddy face.
I do not realize that now suddenly I am old.
With joy I see the Spring wind return.
It is a pity that we must part, but let us make the best of
it and be happy.
We walk to and fro among the peach-trees and plum-trees.
We look at the flowers and drink excellent wine.
We listen to the birds and climb a little way up the bright
hills.
Soon evening comes and the bamboo grove is silent.
There is no one—I shut my door.

AMY LOWELL

18

A Song of Ch'ang-kan

(*Written to Music*)

MY hair had hardly covered my forehead.
I was picking flowers, playing by my door,
When you, my lover, on a bamboo horse,
Came trotting in circles and throwing green plums.

We lived near together on a lane in Chʻang-kan,
Both of us young and happy-hearted.
. . . At fourteen I became your wife,
So bashful that I dared not smile,
And I lowered my head towards a dark corner
And would not turn to your thousand calls;
But at fifteen I straightened my brows and laughed,
Learning that no dust could ever seal our love,
That even unto death I would await you by my post
And would never lose heart in the tower of silent watching.
. . . Then when I was sixteen, you left on a long journey
Through the Gorges of Chʻü-tʻang, of rock and whirling
    water.
And then came the Fifth-month, more than I could bear,
And I tried to hear the monkeys in your lofty far-off sky.
Your footprints by our door, where I had watched you go,
Were hidden, every one of them, under green moss,
Hidden under moss too deep to sweep away.
And the first autumn wind added fallen leaves.
And now, in the Eighth-month, yellowing butterflies
Hover, two by two, in our west-garden grasses. . . .
And, because of all this, my heart is breaking
And I fear for my bright cheeks, lest they fade.
. . . Oh, at last, when you return through the three Pa
    districts,
Send me a message home ahead!
And I will come and meet you and will never mind the
    distance,
All the way to Chang-fêng Sha.

WITTER BYNNER

19

Tears

A FAIR girl draws the blind aside
  And sadly sits with drooping head;
I see her burning tear-drops glide
  But know not why those tears are shed.

H. A. GILES

20

Night Thoughts

I WAKE, the moonbeams play around my bed,
Glittering like hoar-frost to my wondering eyes;
Up towards the glorious moon I raise my head,
Then lay me down—and thoughts of home arise.

H. A. GILES

21

Bringing in the Wine

(Written to Music)

SEE how the Yellow River's waters move out of heaven.
Entering the ocean, never to return.
See how lovely locks in bright mirrors in high chambers,
Though silken-black at morning, have changed by night
  to snow.

. . . Oh, let a man of spirit venture where he pleases
And never tip his golden cup empty towards the moon!
Since heaven gave the talent, let it be employed!
Spin a thousand pieces of silver, all of them come back!
Cook a sheep, kill a cow, whet the appetite,
And make me, of three hundred bowls, one long drink!
. . . To the old master, Ts'ên,
And the young scholar, Tan-ch'iu,
Bring in the wine!
Let your cups never rest!
Let me sing you a song!
Let your ears attend!
What are bell and drum, rare dishes and treasure?
Let me be for ever drunk and never come to reason!
Sober men of olden days and sages are forgotten,
And only the great drinkers are famous for all time.
. . . Prince Ch'ên paid at a banquet in the Palace of Perfection
Ten thousand coins for a cask of wine, with many a laugh and quip.
Why say, my host, that your money is gone?
Go and buy wine and we'll drink it together!
My flower-dappled horse,
My furs worth a thousand,
Hand them to the boy to exchange for good wine,
And we'll drown away the woes of ten thousand generations!

WITTER BYNNER

22

Hard Roads in Shu
(*Written to Music*)

OH, but it is high and very dangerous!
Such travelling is harder than scaling the blue sky.
. . . Until two rulers of this region
Pushed their way through in the misty ages,
Forty-eight thousand years had passed
With nobody arriving across the Ch'in border.
And the Great White Mountain, westward, still has only
a bird's path
Up to the summit of O-mêi Peak—
Which was broken once by an earthquake and there were
brave men lost,
Just finishing the stone rungs of their ladder towards
heaven.
. . . High, as on a tall flag, six dragons drive the sun,
While the river, far below, lashes its twisted course.
Such height would be hard going for even a yellow crane,
So pity the poor monkeys who have only paws to use.
The Mountain of Green Clay is formed of many circles—
Each hundred steps, we have to turn nine turns among
its mounds.
Panting, we brush Orion and pass the Well Star,
Then, holding our chests with our hands and sinking to
the ground with a groan,
We wonder if this westward trail will never have an end.
The formidable path ahead grows darker, darker still,

With nothing heard but the call of birds hemmed in by
the ancient forest,
Male birds smoothly wheeling, following the females;
And there come to us the melancholy voices of the
cuckoos
Out on the empty mountain, under the lonely moon . . .
Such travelling is harder than scaling the blue sky.
Even to hear of it turns the cheek pale,
With the highest crag barely a foot below heaven.
Dry pines hang, head down, from the face of the cliffs,
And a thousand plunging cataracts outroar one another
And send through ten thousand valleys a thunder of
spinning stones.
With all this danger upon danger,
Why do people come here who live at a safe distance?
. . . Though Dagger-Tower Pass be firm and grim,
And while one man guards it
Ten thousand cannot force it,
What if he be not loyal,
But a wolf towards his fellows?
. . . There are ravenous tigers to fear in the day
And venomous reptiles in the night
With their teeth and their fangs ready
To cut people down like hemp.
. . . Though the City of Silk be delectable, I would rather
turn home quickly.
Such travelling is harder than scaling the blue sky . . .
But I still face westward with a dreary moan.

WITTER BYNNER

23

The River Village

THE river makes a bend and encircles the village with its current.
All the long Summer, the affairs and occupations of the river village are quiet and simple.
The swallows who nest in the beams go and come as they please.
The gulls in the middle of the river enjoy one another, they crowd together and touch one another.
My old wife paints a chess-board on paper.
My little sons hammer needles to make fish-hooks.
I have many illnesses, therefore my only necessities are medicines;
Besides these, what more can so humble a man as I ask?

AMY LOWELL

24

The Thatched House unroofed by an Autumn Gale

IT is the Eighth Month, the very height of the Autumn.
The wind rages and roars.
It tears off three layers of my grass-roof.
The thatch flies—it crosses the river—it is scattered about in the open spaces by the river.

High-flying, it hangs, tangled and floating, from the tops of forest trees;
Low-flying, it whirls—turns—and sinks into the hollow of the marsh.
The swarm of small boys from the South Village laugh at me because I am old and feeble.
How dare they act like thieves and robbers before my face,
Openly seizing my thatch and running into my bamboo grove?
My lips are scorched, my mouth dry, I scream at them, but to no purpose.
I return, leaning on my staff. I sigh and breathe heavily.

Presently, of a sudden, the wind ceases. The clouds are the colour of ink.
The Autumn sky is endless—endless—stretching towards dusk and night.
My old cotton quilt is as cold as iron;
My restless son sleeps a troubled sleep, his moving foot tears the quilt.
Over the head of the bed is a leak. Not a place is dry.
The rain streams and stands like hemp—there is no break in its falling.
Since this misery and confusion, I have scarcely slept or dozed.
All the long night I am soaking wet. When will the light begin to sift in?
If I could have a great house of one thousand, ten thousand rooms—

A great shelter where all the Empire's shivering scholars could have happy faces—
Not moved by wind or rain, solid as a mountain—
Alas! When shall I see that house standing before my eyes?
Then, although my own hut were destroyed, although I might freeze and die, I should be satisfied.

AMY LOWELL

25

A Desultory Visit to the Fêng Hsien Temple at the Dragon's Gate

I HAD already wandered away from the People's Temple,
But I was obliged to sleep within the temple precincts.
The dark ravine was full of the music of silence,
The moon scattered bright shadows through the forest.
The Great Gate against the sky seemed to impinge upon the path of the planets.
Sleeping among the clouds, my upper garments, my lower garments were cold.
Wishing to wake, I heard the sunrise bell
Commanding men to come forth and examine themselves in meditation.

AMY LOWELL

26

To My Retired Friend Wêi

It is almost as hard for friends to meet
As for the morning and evening stars.
Tonight then is a rare event,
Joining, in the candlelight,
Two men who were young not long ago
But now are turning grey at the temples.
. . . To find that half our friends are dead
Shocks us, burns our hearts with grief.
We little guessed it would be twenty years
Before I could visit you again.
When I went away, you were still unmarried;
But now these boys and girls in a row
Are very kind to their father's old friend.
They ask me where I have been on my journey;
And then, when we have talked awhile,
They bring and show me wines and dishes,
Spring chives cut in the night-rain
And brown rice cooked freshly a special way.
. . . My host proclaims it a festival,
He urges me to drink ten cups—
But what ten cups could make me as drunk
As I always am with your love in my heart?
. . . Tomorrow the mountains will separate us;
After tomorrow—who can say?

WITTER BYNNER

27

A Song of War-Chariots

(Written to Music)

THE war-chariots rattle,
The war-horses whinny.
Each man of you has a bow and a quiver at his belt.
Father, mother, son, wife, stare at you going,
Till dust shall have buried the bridge beyond Chʻang-an.
They run with you, crying, they tug at your sleeves,
And the sound of their sorrow goes up to the clouds;
And every time a bystander asks you a question,
You can only say to him that you have to go.
. . . We remember others at fifteen sent north to guard the river
And at forty sent west to cultivate the camp-farms.
The mayor wound their turbans for them when they started out.
With their turbaned hair white now, they are still at the border,
At the border where the blood of men spills like the sea—
And still the heart of Emperor Wu is beating for war.
. . . Do you know that, east of China's mountains, in two hundred districts
And in thousands of villages, nothing grows but weeds,
And though strong women have bent to the ploughing,
East and west the furrows all are broken down?
. . . Men of China are able to face the stiffest battle,
But their officers drive them like chickens and dogs.

Whatever is asked of them,
Dare they complain?
For example, this winter
Held west of the gate,
Challenged for taxes,
How could they pay?
. . . We have learned that to have a son is bad luck—
It is very much better to have a daughter
Who can marry and live in the house of a neighbour,
While under the sod we bury our boys.
. . . Go to the Blue Sea, look along the shore
At all the old white bones forsaken—
New ghosts are wailing there now with the old,
Loudest in the dark sky of a stormy day.

WITTER BYNNER

YÜAN CHIEH (723–72)

28

Stone Fish Lake

I LOVED you dearly, Stone Fish Lake,
With your rock-island shaped like a swimming fish!
On the fish's back is the Wine-cup Hollow
And round the fish—the flowing waters of the Lake.
The boys on the shore sent little wooden ships,
Each made to carry a single cup of wine.
The island-drinkers emptied the liquor-boats
And set their sails and sent them back for more.

On the shores of the Lake were jutting slabs of rock
And under the rocks there flowed an icy stream.
Heated with wine, to rinse our mouths and hands
In those cold waters was a joy beyond compare!

Of gold and jewels I have not any need;
For Caps and Coaches I do not care at all.
But I wish I could sit on the rocky banks of the Lake
For ever and ever staring at the Stone Fish.

ARTHUR WALEY

HAN YÜ (A.D. 768–824)

29

Discontent

To stand upon the river-bank and snare the purple fish,
My net well cast across the stream, *was* all that I could wish.
Or lie concealed and shoot the geese that scream and pass apace,
And pay my rents and taxes with the profits of the chase.
Then home to peace and happiness, with wife and children gay,
Though clothes be coarse and fare be hard, and earned from day to day.
But now I read and read, scarce knowing what 'tis all about,
And eager to improve my mind I wear my body out.

I draw a snake and give it legs, to find I've wasted skill,
And my hair grows daily whiter as I hurry towards the hill.
I sit amid the sorrows I have brought on my own head,
And find myself estranged from all, among the living dead.
I seek to drown my consciousness in wine, alas! in vain:
Oblivion passes quickly and my griefs begin again.
Old age comes on and yet withholds the summons to depart. . . .
So I'll take another bumper just to ease my aching heart.

H. A. GILES

30

A Poem on the Stone Drums

CHANG handed me this tracing, from the stone drums,
Beseeching me to write a poem on the stone drums.
Tu Fu has gone. Li Po is dead.
What can my poor talent do for the stone drums?
. . . When the Chou power waned and China was bubbling,
Emperor Hsüan, up in wrath, waved his holy spear
And opened his Great Audience, receiving all the tributes
Of kings and lords who came to him with a tune of clanging weapons.
They held a hunt in Ch'i-yang and proved their marksmanship:

Fallen birds and animals were strewn three thousand miles.
And the exploit was recorded, to inform new generations . . .
Cut out of jutting cliffs, these drums made of stone —
On which poets and artisans, all of the first order,
Had indited and chiselled—were set in the deep mountains
To be washed by rain, baked by sun, burned by wildfire,
Eyed by evil spirits, and protected by the gods.
. . . Where can he have found the tracing on this paper?—
True to the original, not altered by a hair,
The meaning deep, the phrases cryptic, difficult to read,
And the style of the characters neither square nor tadpole.
Time has not yet vanquished the beauty of these letters—
Looking like sharp daggers that pierce live crocodiles,
Like phoenix-mates dancing, like angels hovering down,
Like trees of jade and coral with interlocking branches,
Like golden cord and iron chain tied together tight,
Like incense-tripods flung in the sea, like dragons mounting heaven.
Historians, gathering ancient poems, forgot to gather these,
To make the two Books of Musical Song more colourful and striking;
Confucius journeyed in the west, but not to the Ch'in Kingdom,
He chose our planet and our stars but missed the sun and moon . . .
I who am fond of antiquity, was born too late

And, thinking of these wonderful things, cannot hold back my tears . . .
I remember, when I was awarded my highest degree,
During the first year of Yüan-ho,
How a friend of mine, then at the western camp,
Offered to assist me in removing these old relics.
I bathed and changed, then made my plea to the college president
And urged on him the rareness of these most precious things.
They could be wrapped in rugs, be packed and sent in boxes
And carried on only a few camels: ten stone drums
To grace the Imperial Temple like the Incense-Pot of Kao—
Or their lustre and their value would increase a hundred-fold,
If the monarch would present them to the university,
Where students could study them and doubtless decipher them,
And multitudes, attracted to the capital of culture
From all corners of the Empire, would be quick to gather.
We could scour the moss, pick out the dirt, restore the original surface,
And lodge them in a fitting and secure place for ever,
Covered by a massive building with wide eaves
Where nothing more might happen to them as it had before.
. . . But government officials grow fixed in their ways
And never will initiate beyond old precedent;

THE LIBRARY
COLBY JUNIOR COLLEGE
NEW LONDON, N. H.
27[illegible]

So herd-boys strike the drums for fire, cows polish horns on them,
With no one to handle them reverentially.
Still ageing and decaying, soon they may be effaced.
Six years I have sighed for them, chanting toward the west . . .
The familiar script of Wang Hsi-chih, beautiful though it was,
Could be had, several pages, just for a few white geese!
But now, eight dynasties after the Chou, and all the wars over,
Why should there be nobody caring for these drums?
The Empire is at peace, the government free.
Poets again are honoured and Confucians and Mencians . . .
Oh, how may this petition be carried to the throne?
It needs indeed an eloquent flow, like a cataract—
But, alas, my voice has broken, in my song of the stone drums,
To a sound of supplication choked with its own tears.

WITTER BYNNER

31

Mountain-stones

Rough were the mountain-stones, and the path very narrow;
And when I reached the temple, bats were in the dusk.
I climbed to the hall, sat on the steps, and drank the rain-washed air

Among the round gardenia-pods and huge banana-leaves.
On the old wall, said the priest, were Buddhas finely painted,
And he brought a light and showed me, and I called them wonderful.
He spread the bed, dusted the mats, and made my supper ready,
And, though the food was coarse, it satisfied my hunger.
At midnight, while I lay there not hearing even an insect,
The mountain moon with her pure light entered my door . . .
At dawn I left the mountain, and, alone, lost my way:
In and out, up and down, while a heavy mist
Made brook and mountain green and purple, brightening everything.
I am passing sometimes pines and oaks, which ten men could not girdle,
I am treading pebbles barefoot in swift-running water—
Its ripples purify my ear, while a soft wind blows my garments . . .
These are the things which, in themselves, make life happy.
Why should we be hemmed about and hampered with people?
O chosen pupils, far behind me in my own country,
What if I spent my old age here and never went back home?

WITTER BYNNER

32

On the Festival of the Moon

(To Sub-Official Chang)

THE fine clouds have opened and the River of Stars is gone,
A clear wind blows across the sky, and the moon widens its wave,
The sand is smooth, the water still, no sound and no shadow,
As I offer you a cup of wine, asking you to sing.
But so sad is this song of yours and so bitter your voice
That before I finish listening my tears have become a rain:
'Where Lake Tung-t'ing is joined to the sky by the lofty Nine-doubt Mountain,
Dragons, crocodiles, rise and sink, apes, flying foxes, whimper. . . .
At a ten to one risk of death, I have reached my official post,
Where lonely I live and hushed, as though I were in hiding.
I leave my bed, afraid of snakes; I eat, fearing poisons;
The air of the lake is putrid, breathing its evil odours . . .
Yesterday, by the district office, the great drum was announcing
The crowning of an emperor, a change in the realm.
The edict granting pardons runs three hundred miles a day,
All those who were to die have had their sentences commuted,
The unseated are promoted and exiles are recalled,
Corruptions are abolished, clean officers appointed.

My superior sent my name in, but the governor would
not listen
And has only transferred me to this barbaric place.
My rank is very low and useless to refer to;
They might punish me with lashes in the dust of the street.
Most of my fellow exiles are now returning home—
A journey which, to me, is a heaven beyond climbing.'
. . . Stop your song, I beg you, and listen to mine,
A song that is utterly different from yours:
'To-night is the loveliest moon of the year.
All else is with fate, not ours to control;
But, refusing this wine, may we choose more tomorrow?'

WITTER BYNNER

LIU TSUNG-YÜAN (A.D. 773–819)

33

Reading Buddhist Classics with Ch'ao at His Temple in the Early Morning

I CLEAN my teeth in water drawn from a cold well;
And while I brush my clothes, I purify my mind;
Then, slowly turning pages in the Tree-leaf Book,
I recite, along the path to the eastern shelter.
. . . The world has forgotten the true fountain of this
teaching
And people enslave themselves to miracles and fables.
Under the given words I want the essential meaning,
I look for the simplest way to sow and reap my nature.

Here in the quiet of the priest's temple-courtyard,
Mosses add their climbing colour to the thick bamboo;
And now comes the sun, out of mist and fog,
And pines that seem to be new-bathed;
And everything is gone from me, speech goes, and reading,
Leaving the single unison.

WITTER BYNNER

PO CHÜ-I (A.D. 772–846)

34

A Song of Unending Sorrow

CHINA'S Emperor, craving beauty that might shake an empire,
Was on the throne, for many years, searching, never finding,
Till a little child of the Yang clan, hardly even grown,
Bred in an inner chamber, with no one knowing her,
But with graces granted by heaven and not to be concealed,
At last one day was chosen for the imperial household.
If she but turned her head and smiled, there were cast a hundred spells,
And the powder and paint of the Six Palaces faded into nothing.
. . . It was early spring. They bathed her in the Flower-Pure Pool,

Which warmed and smoothed the creamy-tinted crystal of her skin,
And, because of her langour, a maid was lifting her
When first the Emperor noticed her and chose her for his bride.
The cloud of her hair, petal of her cheek, gold ripples of her crown when she moved,
Were sheltered on spring evenings by warm hibiscus-curtains;
But nights of spring were short and the sun arose too soon,
And the Emperor, from that time forth, forsook his early hearings
And lavished all his time on her with feasts and revelry,
His mistress of the spring, his despot of the night.
There were other ladies in his court, three thousand of rare beauty,
But his favours to three thousand were concentered in one body.
By the time she was dressed in her Golden Chamber, it would be almost evening;
And when tables were cleared in the Tower of Jade, she would loiter, slow with wine.
Her sisters and her brothers all were given titles;
And, because she so illumined and glorified her clan,
She brought to every father, every mother through the empire,
Happiness when a girl was born rather than a boy.
. . . High rose Li Palace, entering blue clouds,
And far and wide the breezes carried magical notes
Of soft song and slow dance, of string and bamboo music.

The Emperor's eyes could never gaze on her enough—
Till war-drums, booming from Yü-yang, shocked the
whole earth
And broke the tunes of *The Rainbow Skirt and the Feathered Coat*.
The Forbidden City, the nine-tiered palace, loomed in the
dust
From thousands of horses and chariots headed south-west.
The imperial flag opened the way, now moving and now
pausing—
But thirty miles from the capital, beyond the western gate,
The men of the army stopped, not one of them would stir
Till under their horses' hoofs they might trample those
moth-eyebrows . . .
Flowery hairpins fell to the ground, no one picked them
up,
And a green and white jade hair-tassel and a yellow-gold
hair-bird.
The Emperor could not save her, he could only cover his
face.
And later when he turned to look, the place of blood and
tears
Was hidden in a yellow dust blown by a cold wind.
. . . At the cleft of the Dagger-Tower Trail they criss-
crossed through a cloud-line
Under O-mêi Mountain. The last few came.
Flags and banners lost their colour in the fading sun-
light . . .
But as waters of Shu are always green and its mountains
always blue,

So changeless was His Majesty's love and deeper than the days.
He stared at the desolate moon from his temporary palace.
He heard bell-notes in the evening rain, cutting at his breast.
And when heaven and earth resumed their round and the dragon-car faced home,
The Emperor clung to the spot and would not turn away
From the soil along the Ma-wêi slope, under which was buried
That memory, that anguish. Where was her jade-white face?
Ruler and lords, when eyes would meet, wept upon their coats
As they rode, with loose rein, slowly eastward, back to the capital.
. . . The pools, the gardens, the palace, all were just as before,
The Lake T'ai-yi hibiscus, the Wêi-yang Palace willows;
But a petal was like her face and a willow-leaf her eyebrow—
And what could he do but cry whenever he looked at them?
. . . Peach-trees and plum-trees blossomed, in the winds of spring;
Lakka-foliage fell to the ground, after autumn rains;
The Western and Southern Palaces were littered with late grasses,
And the steps were mounded with red leaves that no one swept away.

Her Pear-garden Players became white haired
And the eunuchs thin-eyebrowed in her Court of Pepper-Trees;
Over the throne flew fire-flies, while he brooded in the twilight.
He would lengthen the lamp-wick to its end and still could never sleep.
Bell and drum would slowly toll the dragging night-hours
And the River of Stars grow sharp in the sky, just before dawn,
And the porcelain mandarin-ducks on the roof grow thick with morning frost
And his covers of kingfisher-blue feel lonelier and colder
With the distance between life and death year after year;
And yet no beloved spirit ever visited his dreams.
. . . At Ling-ch'ün lived a Taoist priest who was a guest of heaven,
Able to summon spirits by his concentrated mind.
And people were so moved by the Emperor's constant brooding
That they besought the Taoist priest to see if he could find her.
He opened his way in space and clove the ether like lightning,
Up to heaven, under the earth, looking everywhere.
Above, he searched the Green Void, below, the Yellow Spring;
But he failed, in either place, to find the one he looked for.
And then he heard accounts of an enchanted isle at sea,

A part of the intangible and incorporeal world,
With pavilions and fine towers in the five-coloured air,
And of exquisite immortals moving to and fro,
And of one among them—whom they called The Ever
True—
With a face of snow and flowers resembling hers he sought.
So he went to the West Hall's gate of gold and knocked
at the jasper door
And asked a girl, called Morsel-of-Jade, to tell The
Doubly-Perfect.
And the lady, at news of an envoy from the Emperor of
China,
Was startled out of dreams in her nine-flowered canopy.
She pushed aside her pillow, dressed, shook away sleep,
And opened the pearly shade and then the silver screen.
Her cloudy hair-dress hung on one side because of her
great haste,
And her flower-cap was loose when she came along the
terrace,
While a light wind filled her cloak and fluttered with her
motion
As though she danced *The Rainbow Skirt and the Feathered
Coat*.
And the tear-drops drifting down her sad white face
Were like a rain in spring on the blossom of the pear.
But love glowed deep within her eyes when she bade him
thank her liege,
Whose form and voice had been strange to her ever since
their parting—
Since happiness had ended at the Court of the Bright Sun,

And moons and dawns had become long in Fairy-Mountain Palace.
But when she turned her face and looked down toward the earth
And tried to see the capital, there were only fog and dust.
So she took out, with emotion, the pledges he had given
And, through his envoy, sent him back a shell box and gold hairpin,
But kept one branch of the hairpin, and one side of the box,
Breaking the gold of the hairpin, breaking the shell of the box;
'Our souls belong together,' she said, 'like this gold and this shell—
Somewhere, sometime, on earth or in heaven, we shall surely meet.'
And she sent him, by his messenger, a sentence reminding him
Of vows which had been known only to their two hearts:
'On the seventh day of the Seventh-month, in the Palace of Long Life,
We told each other secretly in the quiet midnight world
That we wished to fly in heaven, two birds with the wings of one,
And to grow together on the earth, two branches of one tree.'
. . . Earth endures, heaven endures; sometime both shall end,
While this unending sorrow goes on and on for ever.

WITTER BYNNER

35
The Song of a Guitar

(In the tenth year of Yuan-ho I was banished and demoted to be assistant official in Kiu-kiang. In the summer of the next year I was seeing a friend leave P'ên-p'u and heard in the midnight from a neighbouring boat a guitar played in the manner of the capital. Upon inquiry, I found that the player had formerly been a dancing-girl there and in her maturity had been married to a merchant. I invited her to my boat to have her play for us. She told me her story, heyday and then unhappiness. Since my departure from the capital I had not felt sad; but that night, after I left her, I began to realize my banishment. And I wrote this long poem—six hundred and twelve characters.)

I WAS bidding a guest farewell, at night on the Hsün-yang River,
Where maple-leaves and full-grown rushes rustled in the autumn.
I, the host, had dismounted, my guest had boarded his boat,
And we raised our cups and wished to drink—but, alas, there was no music.
For all we had drunk we felt no joy and were parting from each other,
When the river widened mysteriously towards the full moon—
We had heard a sudden sound, a guitar across the water.
Host forgot to turn back home, and guest to go his way.

We followed where the melody led and asked the player's name.
The sound broke off . . . then reluctantly she answered.
We moved our boat near hers, invited her to join us,
Summoned more wine and lanterns to recommence our banquet.
Yet we called and urged a thousand times before she started toward us,
Still hiding half her face from us behind her guitar.
. . . She turned the tuning-pegs and tested several strings;
We could feel what she was feeling, even before she played:
Each string a meditation, each note a deep thought,
As if she were telling us the ache of her whole life.
She knit her brows, flexed her fingers, then began her music,
Little by little letting her heart share everything with ours.
She brushed the strings, twisted them slow, swept them, plucked them—
First the air of *The Rainbow Skirt*, then *The Six Little Ones*.
The large strings hummed like rain,
The small strings whispered like a secret,
Hummed, whispered—and then were intermingled
Like a pouring of large and small pearls into a plate of jade.
We heard an oriole, liquid, hidden among flowers.
We heard a brook bitterly sob along a bank of sand . . .
By the checking of its cold touch, the very string seemed broken
As though it could not pass; and the notes, dying away

Into a depth of sorrow and concealment of lament,
Told even more in silence than they had told in sound . . .
A silver vase abruptly broke with a gush of water,
And out leapt armoured horses and weapons that clashed
and smote—
And, before she laid her pick down, she ended with one
stroke,
And all four strings made one sound, as of rending silk . . .
There was quiet in the east boat and quiet in the west,
And we saw the white autumnal moon enter the river's
heart.
. . . When she had slowly placed the pick back among
the strings,
She rose and smoothed her clothing and, formal, cour-
teous,
Told us how she had spent her girlhood at the capital,
Living in her parents' house under the Mount of Toads,
And had mastered the guitar at the age of thirteen,
With her name recorded first in the class-roll of musicians,
Her art the admiration even of experts,
Her beauty the envy of all the leading dancers,
How noble youths of Wu-ling had lavishly competed
And numberless red rolls of silk been given for one song,
And silver combs with shell inlay been snapped by her
rhythms,
And skirts the colour of blood been spoiled with stains
of wine . . .
Season after season, joy had followed joy,
Autumn moons and spring winds had passed without
her heeding,

Till first her brother left for the war, and then her aunt died,
And evenings went and evenings came, and her beauty faded—
With ever fewer chariots and horses at her door;
So that finally she gave herself as wife to a merchant
Who, prizing money first, careless how he left her,
Had gone, a month before, to Fou-liang to buy tea.
And she had been tending an empty boat at the river's mouth,
No company but the bright moon and the cold water.
And sometimes in the deep of night she would dream of her triumphs
And be wakened from her dreams by the scalding of her tears.
. . . Her very first guitar-note had started me sighing;
Now, having heard her story, I was sadder still.
'We are both uphappy—to the sky's end.
We meet. We understand. What does acquaintance matter?
I came, a year ago, away from the capital
And am now a sick exile here in Kiu-kiang—
And so remote is Kiu-kiang that I have heard no music,
Neither string nor bamboo, for a whole year.
My quarters, near the River Town, are low and damp,
With bitter reeds and yellowed rushes all about the house.
And what is to be heard here, morning and evening?—
The bleeding cry of cuckoos, the whimpering of apes.
On flowery spring mornings and moonlit autumn nights
I have often taken wine up and drunk it all alone,

Of course there are the mountain songs and the village pipes,
But they are crude and strident, and grate on my ears.
And tonight, when I heard you playing your guitar,
I felt as if my hearing were bright with fairy-music.
Do not leave us. Come, sit down. Play for us again.
And I will write a long song concerning a guitar.'
. . . Moved by what I said, she stood there for a moment,
Then sat again to her strings—and they sounded even sadder,
Although the tunes were different from those she had played before . . .
The feasters, all listening, covered their faces.
But who of them all was crying the most?
This Kiu-kiang official. My blue sleeve was wet.

WITTER BYNNER

36

Hearing the Early Oriole

(*Written in exile*)

When the sun rose I was still lying in bed;
An early oriole sang on the roof of my house.
For a moment I thought of the Royal Park at dawn
When the Birds of Spring greeted their Lord from his trees.
I remembered the days when I served before the Throne
Pencil in hand, on duty at the Ch'eng-ming;

At the height of spring, when I paused an instant from work,
Morning and evening, was *this* the voice I heard?
Now in my exile the oriole sings again
In the dreary stillness of Hsün-yang town . . .
The bird's note cannot really have changed;
All the difference lies in the listener's heart.
If he could but forget that he lives at the world's end,
The bird would sing as it sang in the Palace of old.

ARTHUR WALEY

37

Dreaming that I went with Li and Yü to visit Yüan Chên

(*Written in exile*)

AT night I dreamt I was back in Chʻang-an;
I saw again the faces of old friends.
And in my dreams, under an April sky,
They led me by the hand to wander in the spring winds.
Together we came to the village of Peace and Quiet,
We stopped our horses at the gate of Yüan Chên.
Yüan Chên was sitting all alone;
When he saw me coming, a smile came to his face.
He pointed back at the flowers in the western court;
Then opened wine in the northern summer-house.
He seemed to be saying that neither of us had changed;
He seemed to be regretting that joy will not stay;

That our souls had met only for a little while,
To part again with hardly time for greeting.
I woke up and thought him still at my side;
I put out my hand; there was nothing there at all.

ARTHUR WALEY

38

Pruning Trees

TREES growing—right in front of my window;
The trees are high and the leaves grow thick.
Sad alas! the distant mountain view
Obscured by this, dimly shows between.
One morning I took knife and axe;
With my own hand I lopped the branches off.
Ten thousand leaves fall about my head;
A thousand hills came before my eyes,
Suddenly, as when clouds or mists break
And straight through, the blue sky appears;
Again, like the face of a friend one has loved
Seen at last after an age of parting.
First there came a gentle wind blowing;
One by one the birds flew back to the tree.
To ease my mind I gazed to the South East;
As my eyes wandered, my thoughts went far away.
Of men there is none that has not some preference;
Of things there is none but mixes good with ill.
It was not that I did not love the tender branches;
But better still,—to see the green hills!

ARTHUR WALEY

39

The Cranes

(A.D. 830)

The western wind has blown but a few days;
Yet the first leaf already flies from the bough.
On the drying paths I walk in my thin shoes;
In the first cold I have donned my quilted coat.
Through shallow ditches the floods are clearing away;
Through sparse bamboos trickles a slanting light.
In the early dusk, down an alley of green moss,
The garden-boy is leading the cranes home.

ARTHUR WALEY

40

A Dream of Mountaineering

(*Written when he was over seventy*)

At night, in my dream, I stoutly climbed a mountain,
Going out alone with my staff of holly-wood.
A thousand crags, a hundred hundred valleys—
In my dream-journey none were unexplored
And all the while my feet never grew tired
And my step is as strong as in my young days.
Can it be that when the mind travels backward
The body also returns to its old state?
And can it be, as between body and soul,

That the body may languish, while the soul is still strong?
Soul and body—both are vanities:
Dreaming and waking—both alike unreal.
In the day my feet are palsied and tottering;
In the night my steps go striding over the hills.
As day and night are divided in equal parts—
Between the two, I *get* as much as I *lose*.

ARTHUR WALEY

YÜAN CHÊN (A.D. 779–831)

41

The Pitcher

I DREAMT I climbed to a high, high plain;
And on the plain I found a deep well.
My throat was dry with climbing and I longed to drink,
And my eyes were eager to look into the cool shaft.
I walked round it; I looked right down;
I saw my image mirrored on the face of the pool.
An earthen pitcher was sinking into the black depths;
There was no rope to pull it to the well-head.
I was strangely troubled lest the pitcher should be lost,
And started wildly running to look for help.
From village to village I scoured that high plain;
The men were gone: the dogs leapt at my throat.
I came back and walked weeping round the well;
Faster and faster the blinding tears flowed—
Till my own sobbing suddenly woke me up;

My room was silent, no one in the house stirred;
The flame of my candle flickered with a green smoke;
The tears I had shed glittered in the candle-light.
A bell sounded; I knew it was the midnight chime;
I sat up in bed and tried to arrange my thoughts:
The plain in my dream was the graveyard at Chʻang-an,
Those hundred acres of untilled land.
The soil heavy and the mounds heaped high;
And the dead below them laid in deep troughs.
Deep are the troughs, yet sometimes dead men
Find their way to the world above the grave.
And to-night my love who died long ago
Came into my dream as the pitcher sunk in the well.
That was why the tears suddenly streamed from my eyes,
Streamed from my eyes and fell on the collar of my dress.

ARTHUR WALEY

42

An Elegy

I

O YOUNGEST, best-loved daughter of Hsieh,
Who unluckily married this penniless scholar,
You patched my clothes from your own wicker basket,
And I coaxed off your hairpins of gold, to buy wine with;
For dinner we had to pick wild herbs—
And to use dry locust-leaves for our kindling.
. . . To-day they are paying me a hundred thousand—
And all that I can bring to you is a temple sacrifice.

II

We joked, long ago, about one of us dying,
But suddenly, before my eyes, you are gone.
Almost all your clothes have been given away;
Your needlework is sealed, I dare not look at it . . .
I continue your bounty to our men and our maids—
Sometimes, in a dream, I bring you gifts.
. . . This is a sorrow that all mankind must know—
But not as those know it who have been poor together.

III

I sit here alone, mourning for us both.
How many years do I lack now of my threescore and ten?
There have been better men than I to whom heaven
denied a son,
There was a poet better than I whose dead wife could not
hear him.
What have I to hope for in the darkness of our tomb?
You and I had little faith in a meeting after death—
Yet my open eyes can see all night
That lifelong trouble of your brow.

WITTER BYNNER

LI CHIA-YU (8TH OR 9TH CENTURY A.D.)

43

In Retirement

HE envies none, the pure and proud ex-Minister of State;
On the Western Lake he shuts himself within his bamboo gate.
He needs no fan to cool his brow, for the south wind never lulls,
While idly his official hat lies staring at the gulls.

H. A. GILES

TU MU (A.D. 803–52)

44

The Last Night

OLD love would seem as though not love to-day;
Spell-bound by thee, my laughter dies away.
The very wax sheds sympathetic tears
And gutters sadly down till dawn appears.

H. A. GILES

LI SHÊ (9TH CENTURY A.D.)

45

Escape

CONFUSION overwhelming me, as in drunken dream,
I note that spring has fled and wander off to hill and stream;
With a friendly Buddhist priest I seek a respite from the strife
And manifold anomalies which go to make up life.

H. A. GILES

OU-YANG HSIU (A.D. 1007–72)

46

The Cicada

In the summer of the first year of Chia-yu (A.D. 1056), there was a great flood. By order of the Emperor, I went to the Wine Spring Temple to pray for fine weather, when I heard a cicada singing. Upon which subject I wrote this poem:

HUSHED was the courtyard of the temple;
Solemn stood I, gazing
At the bright roofs and gables,
The glorious summits of that towering shrine.
Untroubled were my thoughts, intently prayed
My fasting soul, for every wandering sense

Was gathered to its home.
Unmoved I watched the motions of the world,
Saw deep into the nature of ten thousand things.
Suddenly the rain was over, no wind stirred
The morning-calm; round all the sky
Was cloudless blue, and the last thunder rolled.
Then we, to strew sweet-scented herbs upon the floor,
Drew near the coloured cloister, by whose side
Some old trees grew amid the grass
Of the deserted court. Here was a thing that cried
Upon a tree-top, sucking the shrill wind
To wail it back in a long whistling note—
That clasping in its arms
A tapering twig perpetually sighed,
Now shrill as flute, now soft as mandolin;
Sometimes a piercing cry
Choked at its very uttering, sometimes a cold tune
Dwindled to silence, then suddenly flowed again,
A single note, wandering in strange keys,
An air, yet fraught
With undertone of secret harmony.
'What creature can this be?' 'Cicada is its name.'
'Are you not he, cicada,
Of whom I have heard told you can transform
Your body, magically moulding it
To new estate? Are you not he who, born
Upon the dung-heap, coveted the sky,
The clean and open air;
Found wings to mount the wind, yet skyward sailing
Upon a leafy tree-top checked your flight,

Pleased with its trim retreat? Are you not he
Who with the dew for drink, the wind for food,
Grows never old nor languid; who with looped locks
Frames womanish beauty?
Long since have I marvelled
How of ten thousand creatures there is not one
But has his tune; how, as each season takes its turn,
A hundred new birds sing, each weather wakes
A hundred insects from their sleep.
Now lisp the mango-birds
Like pretty children, prattling at their play.
As shuttle at the sounding loom
The tireless cricket creaks. Beautiful the flexions
Of tongue and thrilling throat, how valiantly
They spend themselves to do it!
And even the croakers of the pond,
When they get rain to fill
Their miry, parching puddles, while they sip
New rivulets and browse the soppy earth,
Sing through the livelong night. And like enough
May frogs be passionate; but oh, what seeks
The silent worm in song?
These and a thousand others, little and great,
Too many to name them all,
Myriads of creatures—each after his own shape and kin,
Hold at their season ceaseless tournament of song;
But swiftly, swiftly
Their days run out, time transmutes them, and there is
    silence,
Desert silence where they sang.

Alas! philosophy has taught
That the transcending mind in its strange, level world
Sees not kinds, contraries, classes, or degrees.
And if of living things
Man once seemed best, what has he but a knack
Of facile speech, what but a plausible scheme
Of signs and ciphers that perpetuate
His thoughts and phrases? And on these expends
His brooding wits, consumes his vital breath;
One droning out the extremity of his woe,
Another to the wide world publishing
His nobleness of heart!

Thus though he shares
The brief span of all creatures, yet his song
A hundred ages echoes after him.
But you, cicada,
What know you of this? Only for yourself
You make your music . . .'

So was I pondering, comparing,
Setting difference by difference, gain by gain,
When suddenly the clouds came back and overhead
The storm blazed and crashed, spilling huge drops
Out of the rumbling sky . . .

And silent now
Was the cicada's voice.

ARTHUR WALEY

ANONYMOUS (18TH CENTURY)

47

An Agnostic

You ask me why I greet the priest
    But not his God;
The God sits mute, the man at least
    Returns my nod.

H. A. GILES

CHEN SHAN-SHIH (SUNG DYNASTY)

48

The Herd-Boy's Song

SPLASHING water,
Luscious grass;
Somebody's child is herding an ox,
Riding his ox by the river-side.
Browsing ox,
Happy youth;
Somebody's child is singing a song,
Shouting his song to a little white cloud:

    Away at morn my ox I ride,
    And back again at eventide.

    My two feet never touch the dust;
    In wealth and fame who puts his trust?

My rush hat shelters me from rain;
In silk and sables what's to gain?

I quench my thirst at a mountain rill;
Who'd spend a fortune his belly to fill?

When the sun on his golden horse rides high
Down by the river go ox and I;

When the sinking sun makes shadows creep
He carries me home on his back, asleep.

E. D. EDWARDS

49

The Moon in the Mountains

HERE in the mountains the moon I love,
Hanging alight in a distant grove;
Pitying me in my loneliness,
She reaches a finger and touches my dress.
    My heart resembles the moon;
    The moon resembles my heart.
My heart and the moon in each other delight,
Each watching the other throughout the long night.

E. D. EDWARDS

ANONYMOUS

50

Tea-picking Ballad

WHERE a thousand hills the vale enclose, our little hut is there,
And on the sloping sides around, the Tea grows everywhere;
And I must rise at early dawn, as busy as can be,
To get my daily labour done, and pluck the leafy tea.

At early dawn I seize my crate, and sighing, oh, for rest,
Through the thick mist I pass the door, with sloven hair half-drest.
The dames and maidens call to me, as hand in hand they go,
'What slope do you, Miss, climb to-day, what slope of high Sung-lo?'

Dark is the sky, the twilight dim still on the hills is set,
The dewy leaves and cloudy buds may not be gathered yet.
Oh, who are they, the thirsty ones, for whom this work we do;
For whom we spend our daily toil, in bands of two and two?

We aid each other like good friends, and to each other say,
As down we pull the yielding twigs, 'Sweet sister, don't delay;
E'en now the buds are growing old, all on the boughs atop;
And then to-morrow—who can tell?—the drizzling rain may drop.'

We've picked enough, the topmost bough is bare of
 leaves, and so
We lift our brimming loads, and by the homeward path
 we go.
With merry laughter by the pool, the lotus pool, we hie;
When hark! uprise two mallards, and hence affrighted fly.

Limpid and clear the pool, and there how rich the lotus
 grows!
And only half its opening leaves, as round as coins, it shows.
Over the jutting brink I bend, and to myself I say,
Gazing within the glassy stream, 'How looks my face
 to-day?'

My face is dirty, out of trim my hair is, and awry.
Oh tell me where 's the little girl so ugly now as I?
'Tis all because whole weary hours I'm forced to pick
 the tea,
And driving winds and soaking showers have made me
 what you see.

With morn again come wind and rain, and though so
 fierce and strong,
With basket big and little hat I wend my way along;
Then home once more, when all is picked, and everybody
 sees
How muddy all our dresses are, and dabbled to the knees.

I saw this morning through the door a pleasant day set in;
Be sure I quickly drest my hair, and neatly fixed my pin;
And featly down the path I sped to gain the wonted spot,
But, never thinking of the mire, my working shoes forgot!

The garden reached, my bow-shaped shoes are soaking
through and through;
The sky is changed—the thunder rolls—I don't know
what to do.
I'll call my comrades on the hill to pass the word with speed,
And fetch my green umbrella hat, to help me in my need.

But my little hat does little good, my plight is very sad.
I stand with clothes all dripping wet, like some poor
fisher-lad;
Like him I have a basket too of meshes woven fine—
A fisher-lad, if I only had his fishing-rod and line.

The rain is over, the outer leaves their branching fibres
show.
Shake down the branch, and round us fragrant scent
begins to blow.
Gather the yellow golden threads that high and low are
found.
Ah, what a precious odour now is wafted all around!

No sweeter perfume does the wild and fair Aglaia shed;
That *my* tea is the choicest will everywhere be said.
When all are picked we'll leave the shoots to bud again
in spring,
But for this morning we have done the third, last gathering.

Oh weary is our picking; yet my toil I don't withhold.
My maiden locks are all askew, my pearly fingers cold.
I only wish our tea to be superior over all,
O'er this one's 'sparrow-tongue', and o'er the other's
'dragon ball'.

Oh, for a weary month I strive to find a leisure day;
I go to pick at early dawn, and till the dusk I stay.
Till midnight at the firing-pan I keep my irksome place;
But may not labour hard as this impair my pretty face?

But if my face be somewhat lank, more firm shall be my
mind.
I'll fire my tea: all else shall be my golden buds behind.
But yet the thought arises, who the pretty maid shall be,
To put the leaves in jewelled cup, from thence to drink
my tea.

Her griefs all flee as she makes her tea, and she is glad;
but oh
How shall she learn the toils of us who labour for her so?
How shall she know of the winds that blow, and the rains
that pour their wrath,
And drench and soak us through and through, as though
plunged in a bath?

In driving rains and howling winds the birds forsake the
nest;
Yet many a loving pair are seen still on the boughs to rest.
Oh, wherefore, loved one, with light look didst thou
send me away?
I cannot, grieving as I grieve, go through my work today.

But though my bosom rise and fall, like a bucket in a well,
So industrious am I that against my work I'll ne'er rebel.
My care shall be to have my tea fired to a tender brown,
And let the *flag* and *awl*, well rolled, display their whitish
down.

Hah, for my toil, ho, for my steps! Aweary tho' I be,
In our poor house, for working folk, there's lots of work I see.
When the firing and the drying 's done, off at the call I go,
And once again this morning will I climb the high Sung-lo!

My wicker basket slung on arm, and hair entwined with
flowers,
To the slopes I go of the high Sung-lo, and pick the tea
for hours.
How we laugh, sisters, on the road! What a merry turn
we've got!
I giggle and say, as I point down the way, 'There, look,
there lies our cot!

Your handmaid 'neath the sweet green shade in sheltered
cot abides,
Where the pendent willow's sweeping bough the thatchy
dwelling hides.
To-morrow if you wish it so, my guests I pray you'll be,
The door you'll know by the fragrant scent, the scent of
the firing tea.'

Awhile it 's cold, and then it 's warm; when I want to fire
my tea,
The sky is sure to shift and change—and all to worry me.
When the Sun goes down on the western hills, on the
eastern there is rain,
And however fair he promises, he promises in vain.

To-day the western mountains are looking bright and fair,
And I bear my crate to the stile, and wait my fellow-toiler
there:

A little tender lass is she—she leans upon the rail,
And sleeps—and though I hail her, she answers not my
hail.

And when at length to my loudest call she murmurs a reply,
'Tis with sleep not yet conquered, and with half-opened eye;
She starts up, and with straggling steps along the path
she 's gone;
She brings her basket, but forgets to put the cover on!

Together we trudge on and pass the lodge of the southern
bowers,
Where the beautiful sea-pomegranate waves all its yellow
flowers.
Fain would we stop and pluck a few to deck our tresses gay,
But the tree is high, and 'tis vain to try to reach the
tempting spray.

The pretty birds upon the bough sing songs so sweet to hear,
And the sky is so delicious now, half cloudy and half clear.
While bending o'er her work, each maid will prattle of
her woe,
And we talk till our hearts are sad and sore, and tears
unstinted flow.

Our time is up, and yet not full our baskets to the mouth.
The twigs to the north are fully searched, let 's seek them
in the south.
Just then by chance I snapped a twig whose leaves were
all apair;
See, with my taper fingers now I fix it in my hair.

Of all the various kinds of tea, the bitter beats the sweet;
But whoever seeks for either, for him I'll find a treat.
Though who it is shall drink them, whether bitter or
    sweet they be,
I know not, friend—but the pearly end of my finger
    only I see.

Ye twittering swallows rise and fall in your flight round
    the hill;
But when next I go to the high Sung-lo, I'll change my
    gown—I will;
I'll roll up the cuff and show arm enough, for my arm
    is fair to see.
Oh, if ever there were a fair round arm, that arm belongs
    to me!

W. T. MERCER

CH'ÊN MÊNG-CHIA (b. 1911)

51

Still No Dawn

Three times the watchman hobbled on his round,
One, two, three;
His wooden rattle heavily resounded.
Light were the roofs, just four or five,
In the village fast asleep.
I peered outside the window:
Still no dawn.

CHʻEN MÊNG-CHIA

The cock crew several times,
One, two, three.
The stars were sinking,
The world became a sultry river,
The wind blew, fretful, cold.
I peered outside the window:
Still no dawn.

HAROLD ACTON

52

The Song of the Wind-bell

In sunshine or rain,
As floating clouds light,
Like a mountain-grove hermit:
Ding-ding, ding-a-ling.

I pray not to winds
Nor to sprites of the mountain.
When winds blow I tremble,
I cease when winds cease.

Without sorrow,
Without joy,
Forever ancient,
Forever young.

I am a wind-bell
In an old temple,
And the sun smiles to me,
Golden rust grows on me.

Maybe one day
God will silence me.
I shall fly to the heavens
Transformed to a star.

HAROLD ACTON

HÖ CHI-FANG (b. 1911)

53

To a Friend in Winter

When yellow pine-cones fall
And birds are flying low with rustling wings,
You will stop your companionless walks in the wood;
When water 's cold and the fish are hiding,
In the pond will float your lonely fishing-line;
When your casement 's covered with hoar-frost. . . .

For long secluded in illness,
Do you still think of your dwelling in the north?

In the old bamboo chair at the corner of the room
And in the shadows of the walls,
Full many of my cares have taken refuge:
For then I oft had cares

And you oft had gentle silence.
Over the window of ragged gauze
Often the lizards were twitching their grey legs.
Outside in the courtyard
The single shivering sound of the woodpecker
Dripped from the chinks between tiny locust-leaves.
You asked me whether I loved that sound.
If it were now, I would certainly say I love it.

A troop of camels newly befurred in the west wind
Lift up their heavy hooves
And gently pat them down.
The street is coated with thin frost.

HAROLD ACTON

54

Autumn

SCATTERING all the pearly dews of morning,
The noise of timber-felling riddles the deep ravine,
Sickles sated with rice are put aside,
Plump melons and hedgerow-fruits are loaded in baskets.
Autumn lingers about the farm-houses.

Round nets are cast in the chilly mist on the river's brim,
Flat-fish-like shadows of maple-leaves are gathered,
The awnings are covered under films of frost,
As they row homeward gently sway the oars.
Autumn dallies about the fishermen's boats.

With chattering crickets the meadow seems more vast,
With boulders visible the brook more limpid.
Where are the flutes on the backs of oxen,
Whence flowed the heat and scent of summer nights?
Autumn dozes in the eyes of the shepherdess.

HAROLD ACTON

55

A Wreath

(*to be placed on a little tomb*)

MOST fragrant are flowers that bloom and fade in a black ravine,
Brightest are unremembered dew-drops in the dawn.
You I must hail as blessed, little Ling-ling!
Purest the brook that never reflected an image.

You dreamt of green creepers climbing through your window
And of golden flowers falling over your hair.
You were stirred by tales of the rain as it dripped down the eaves,
And the solitary starlight was your love.

Virginal pearls, the tears that often flowed
To clear your heart of all unshapely sorrows.
So beautiful your days, they made you grieve—
More beautiful your early hour of death!

HAROLD ACTON

HSÜ CHIH-MO (1895–1931)

56

Two Moons

Two moons I see,
The same in shape, yet different in feature.

The one 's just in the sky
Decked in a gown of bird-plumes.
She does not stint her favours,
Her gold and silver spread o'er all the earth.
She does not forget the tiles on the palace-roof.
And the Three Lakes brim and glisten with her beauty.
Over the clouds she leaps, over the tree-tops,
And hides herself in green shades of the vine.
She is so delicate and comely
Even the fish within the lakes are rapt!
And yet she has a flaw—
The naughty habit of becoming thin:
Sometimes the sparks of stars are seen aloft
But not her round enchanting countenance.
And though she may return at other seasons
This absence is a torture too excessive.

Another moon there is you cannot see,
Despite the splendour of her radiance.
She also has her dimple-smiles
And grace of movement;
She 's no less generous than the other moon—
What a pity that you cannot see my garden!

Sublime her sorcery,
Kindling and quickening my ecstasies:
I love her sudden swell of silver waves
Lapping with melodies of silver bells,
Even her foam, blown white like horses' tails,
Fostered more tenderly than deep-sea pearls.
A full and perfect moon
Who never wanes.
Whenever I close these eyes of mine
She rises up and sails into the heavens.

HAROLD ACTON

57

The Snow-flake's Delight

If I were a snow-flake
That lightly frolics in the air,
Certainly I would know my destination,
Flit, flit, flit—
There is my destination, down on earth.

I would not go to the lonely secret valley
Nor to the desolate mountain slope,
Nor would I languish in the empty street,
Flit, flit, flit—
You see I really have a destination.

Gracefully I'd fly on through the air
Till I recognized that lovely residence,
There I would wait for her to walk in the garden—
Flit, flit, flit—
Ah, there is the scent of plum-flower around her!

Then with the lightness of my body
I'd delicately cling upon her dress,
Draw nearer to the ripples of her breast,
Melt, melt, melt,
Melt into the soft waves of her breast.

HAROLD ACTON

LIN KÊNG (b. 1910)

58

The Country in Spring

SPRING's blue water gushes down the hill,
Beside the brook the lush grass thickens.
No one remembers, and none can tell
Where winter's wind has gone.
A sound as of a bell at noon,
Soft as the breeze in blossom-time,
Follows the aimless butterfly
Over spring's country.

HAROLD ACTON

59

Autumn

In autumn's woodland heaven is high and bright,
Red plane-leaves strew the ground.
Who has a broom with a long handle
To sweep the fallen leaves on to the path?
A green-clad postman passes through the woodland,
Swiftly the white clouds race above the trees:
Will they fly over the river?
A man who daily pauses in the wood
May lose himself in leafy meditations.

HAROLD ACTON

T'AI WANG-SHU (*c.* 1900)

60

The Unrequited Lover

I fancy that I'm an unrequited lover
But I know not whom I love.
Maybe a land in faint haze by the sea,
Maybe a flower withering in silence,
Maybe some beauty met on a road and then forgotten:
I cannot tell.
As if I were in love
My bosom swells, my heart throbs ever faster.

Tired, I would wander through dark streets,
Wander through all riotous places
And think not to return, as if in search of something.
A floating pin-point of bewitching eye,
Sweet words that touch the ear—
Such incidents are common;
But I would say in a low voice: 'Not you!'
And stagger on elsewhere.

'Night-walker' people call me.
Let them!—it 's all the same to me.
In sooth I am a lonely night-walker,
A lover unrequited.

HAROLD ACTON

61

My Memory

My memory is quite devoted to me,
More devoted than my dearest friends.

It dwells on smouldering cigarettes,
On my lily-patterned penholder,
On a worn-out powder-puff,
On the lichen of broken walls;
It dwells on a bottle of half-drained liquor,
On a torn poem, on a flattened petal,
On lamplight, on calm water,
On all things with a soul or even without one.
My memory dwells everywhere—like me in the world.

T'AI WANG-SHU

It is timid and afraid of people's noise,
But in lonely periods pays me secret visits.
Its voice is soft and low,
But its conversation is exceedingly long
And exceedingly detailed, and never likely to stop:
Its words are old, and always the same tale,
Its voice harmonious, and always the same tune.
Sometimes it mimics the tone of young coquettes,
Its voice is fainter then
And mixed with sobs, with sighs.

Its visits are irregular,
At any time, at any place—
Often when I am dozing off in bed:
Or it may choose an early morning.
Some people might say my memory 's rather rude
But we're old friends.

It is always gossipy, never dreams of pausing
Unless I burst into desolate tears
Or heavily fall asleep.
But I never find it offensive
Because it 's so truly devoted.

HAROLD ACTON

62

The Country Girl

THE country girl she quietly tripped along
Carrying a bucket green with lichen,
Her feet were sprinkled by the splashing water,
Her heart was under the willow by the well.

The girl would quietly walk to her old cottage
Under the centenarian evergreen
But when she thought of the boy who had kissed her by
the well,
She would smile and purse her lips.

Towards her cottage turning,
She would scare to flight a flock of pecking sparrows,
Quietly she would walk into the kitchen
And quietly drop the bucket by the hay.

She would help her mother to prepare the meal
And her father, back from the fields, would sit and
smoke;
She would feed the pigs and drive the fowls to roost.

At dinner in the twilight
Her father would discourse on this year's harvest,
Mutter some words anent his daughter's marriage—
Then, timidly, the girl would bend her head.

T'AI WANG-SHU

Her mother would complain of her laziness
(That dallying by the well was an example)
But she never even heard her mother's speech;
She was thinking the boy had been a little rough.

HAROLD ACTON

NOTES

1–3. It is impossible to know when the poems of the *Book of Songs* were composed or collected. Mr. Waley says that 'Such of the songs as are datable range between 800 and 600 B.C.' Many are probably much older. The first that is here translated is a simple country love-song. In the second song, the phrase 'Only thirty brindled beasts!' implies that the rest are whole-coloured, and therefore suitable for sacrifice. The third is a Dynastic Song of uncertain date.

4–5. Chang Hêng (139–78 B.C.) was a great astronomer and mathematician. The Emperor An Ti, hearing of his fame, summoned him to court and appointed him Grand Historiographer. He wrote a treatise on astronomy, and in A.D. 132 he constructed the first seismograph. There is some doubt whether these two poems were really written by him.

Chuang Tzŭ (No. 4) was the great Taoist philosopher whose works have been translated by H. A. Giles, and in part by Mr. Waley.

6. Wang Yen-shou (*circa* A.D. 130), son of the poet Wang I, was drowned while crossing the Hsiang river, at the age of twenty, or, according to other accounts, of twenty-four.

The Wangsun is supposed to be a small tailless ape.

7. T'ao Ch'ien (A.D. 365–427), after a youth of studious poverty, obtained a post as magistrate, which, however, he only held for 83 days. He found himself unfitted by nature for official life, all he wanted being 'length of days and depth of wine'. So he retired and occupied himself with poetry, music, and the culture of flowers, especially chrysanthemums. Yet in spite of his loathing of restraint, he was compelled at least four times to re-enter official life in order to earn a living. Much of his poetry is of great originality and beauty, and was frequently imitated by later Chinese writers.

10. Wang Wei (A.D. 699–759) was born at T'ai-yüan in Shansi. In his youth he distinguished himself as a musician, and was appointed assistant in the Grand College of Music. Afterwards he was promoted to the post of Junior Censor. At Ch'ang-an he became one of the brilliant group of writers and painters at the court of the Emperor Ming Huang. 'Wang Wei', writes Mr. Waley, 'was the first great poet who was also a great painter. His poems reflect the perfect balance of his nature. Exquisite in their technique, they are more reflective, more personal, and consequently less completely lyrical than those of Li Po. At the same time he wholly lacked the political ardour of Tu Fu. . . . Wang Wei is the most classical of Chinese poets.' He died at Ch'ang-an in 759, four years after the An Lu-shan rebellion, during which he had suffered imprisonment and other hardships. Upon the death of his mother, a devout Buddhist, to whom he was deeply attached, he turned part of his country-house into a monastery in her memory and was buried there.

One *li* was about a fifth of a mile in T'ang times.

12. At the age of thirty-one Wang Wei left his official post and came to live near Mount Chung-nan, fifteen miles south of Ch'ang-an, turning his heart to the teachings of Taoism. Tao, or the Way, meant to the Taoists 'the Way the universe works', something very like God, in an abstract and philosophical sense.

17. Li Po was born in A.D. 701 of well-to-do parents at Pa-hsi in Ssech'uan. At ten he had mastered the Confucian *Book of Odes*, and was writing poems of his own. When he grew up, he retired with a scholarly recluse to the Min Mountains, and even when summoned to the provincial examination he made no response. He was interested in politics and poetry and fond of fencing, 'caring nothing for wealth and much for almsgiving'.

At the age of twenty-five he left the Min Mountains and

lived a wandering life, visiting Shantung and Yun-meng near the Tung-ting Lake. Here he married and lived for a few years, until his wife, impatient of his failure to obtain official promotion, deserted him with the children. About this time he lived on Mount Chʻu Lai in Shantung with five genial companions, who called themselves the Six Idlers of the Bamboo Brook, and spent their time drinking, writing and reciting poems, and playing on the lute. In 742 Li Po went to Chʻang-an, and was there introduced to the Emperor Ming Huang, who, charmed by Po's genius, made him his familiar friend and boon companion. Once, when Po was drunk, the Emperor ordered the powerful eunuch, Kao Li-shih, to take off Po's shoes; an insult for which Li-shih revenged himself by slandering the poet to Yang Kuei-fei, the Emperor's favourite mistress. So the poet retired from Court, and soon afterwards formed a new association of companions, known as the Eight Immortals of the Wine-cup. When he was forty-five, Li Po once more set out on his travels, and wandered about the country for ten years; until in 755 the An Lu-shan rebellion broke out. After various perils and hardships, imprisonment, and a sentence of death commuted to one of banishment to a remote region of the south-west, an amnesty allowed him to return to Kiu-kiang. Finally he went to live with a friend and disciple in the Liu Mountains near Kiu-kiang, where soon afterwards he died, in 762, at the age of 61. There is a legend that he was drowned while leaning over the side of a boat in a drunken effort to embrace the reflection of the moon.

22. The road Li Po is describing runs from Shensi Province (Chʻin) to Ssechʻuan (Shu). 'The City of Silk', Chêng-tu, was the capital of Ssechʻuan.

23. Tu Fu was born in A.D. 713 at Tu Ling in Shensi of very poor parents. Already as a boy he showed great literary talent; yet he failed at his first public examination, because,

we are told, the opinions he expressed in his papers were so radical that the authorities refused to give him a degree. So he took to wandering about the country, observing and writing poetry, with no prospect save a life of poverty. It was not until Tu Fu was forty, and a famous poet, that the Emperor Ming Huang took notice of him, and gave him an official post in the Chieh Hsien library. But soon, in 755, the An Lu-shan rebellion broke out, and, to quote Mr. Waley, 'terminated the most polished epoch that the world had ever seen'. Tu Fu found refuge with a relative in a country village; but after the revolution had been crushed he made his way, starving and in rags, to the Court of the new Emperor, who at once appointed him to the important post of Censor. But the Emperor soon took offence at his imprudent outspokenness, and banished him to a minor official post in Shensi. This post he immediately resigned, and spent most of the rest of his life in wretched poverty, wandering from place to place until he reached Ch'entu in Ssech'uan, where he lived in a grass-roofed house, writing poetry, and 'making the two ends of nothing meet'. A few years later he wandered off again, till he was caught by floods and took refuge in a ruined temple, where after ten days he was discovered in a starving condition. Meat and wine were brought in; but he ate and drank so ravenously after his long fast that he died within an hour.

25. The Fêng Hsien temple is one of those temples built by the people, not by Imperial command. It stands in the Lung Mēn, or Dragon Gate, a defile said to have been cut in the mountains of Honan by the legendary King Yü (2205 B.C.), when he drained the flooded lowland. He is supposed to have been helped by a dragon, who with one sweep of his tail cleft the mountain in two.

28. Yüan Chieh, a contemporary of Li Po, has not hitherto been much noticed in European books. 'His subjects were

always original, but his poems are seldom worth quoting', is a Chinese opinion of him.

29. Han Yü (A.D. 768–824) was a native of Honan, who after a brilliant official career rose to be President of the Board of Rites. In 819 he presented a memorial protesting against the extravagant honours with which the Emperor proposed to receive a bone of Buddha. For this bitter and courageous attack upon the fashionable cult Han Yü was banished to Kwangtung, where he did his best to civilize the rude inhabitants of that remote province. Before long he was recalled to the capital and reinstated in office; but he died soon afterwards at the age of fifty-six. He is perhaps more famous for his prose essays than for his poetry. The Sung poet, Su Tung-po, writes of him that 'from the age of the Hans the Truth began to be obscured and literature to fade. Supernatural religions sprang up on all sides; and many eminent scholars failed to oppose their advance, until Han Yü, the cotton-clothed, arose and blasted them with his derision.'

The Chinese prefer hill-sides for their burying-grounds.

30. Among the oldest-known stone-carvings of the Chinese, these ten stone drums were made, and engraved with poems, under the Emperor Hsuan of the Chou Dynasty. Three of them still exist, and are now in the Confucian Temple at Peking, together with replicas of the other seven.

Examples of Wan Hai-chih's calligraphy even in his own time were very valuable; but he would not sell them, except in exchange for a few white geese, of which he was extremely fond.

34. Po Chü-i was born in A.D. 772 at T'ai-yüan in Shansi. He tells us that his family was poor and often in difficulties. He seems to have settled at Ch'ang-an, the capital of the Empire, in 801. Soon afterwards he met Yüan Chên, then aged twenty-two, who was destined to play so important

a part in his life. In 805 Yüan Chên was banished from the capital, and the separation was a heavy blow to Po Chü-i, who at this period of his life made friends with difficulty, not being, so he tells us, 'a master of such accomplishments as calligraphy, painting, chess or gambling, which tend to bring men together in pleasurable intercourse'. In 804 on the death of his father, and again in 811 on the death of his mother, he spent periods of retirement on the Wei river near Ch'ang-an. Soon after his return to the capital in 814 he fell into official disfavour. In two long memorials entitled 'On Stopping the War', he had criticized the handling of a campaign against an unimportant tribe of Tartars, which he considered had been unduly prolonged. In a series of poems he had satirized the rapacity of minor officials and called attention to the intolerable sufferings of the masses. His enemies, by means of ridiculous insinuations and slanders, soon found an opportunity of silencing him, and he was banished to Kiukiang with the rank of sub-prefect. After three years he was made Governor of Chung-chou, a remote place in Ssech'uan. On the way up the Yangtze he met Yüan Chên after three years of separation. They spent a few days together at I-ch'ang, exploring the rock-caves of the neighbourhood. In 819 he was recalled to the capital and became a second-class Assistant Secretary. In 821, on account of a series of memorials criticizing the Emperor's arbitrary misgovernment, he was again banished, this time to be Governor of the important town of Hangchow. His friend Yüan Chên now held a judicial post at Ningpo, and the two were occasionally able to meet. In 824 his Governorship expired, and he lived for a time at a village near Lo-yang. It was here that he took into his household two girls, Fan-su and Man-tzŭ, whose singing and dancing enlivened his retreat. In 825 he became the Governor of Soochow. Here at the age of fifty-three he enjoyed a kind of second youth, much more sociable than that of thirty years before: we find him endlessly picnicking and feasting. But after two years, illness obliged him to retire. In 829 he settled at Lo-yang as Governor of Honan. In 831 Yüan Chên died; and for the rest of his life Po Chü-i lived a life of retirement. He repaired an unoccupied part of the Hsiang-shan monastery, near Lo-yang, and lived there calling himself the Hermit of Hsiang-shan. In the winter of 839 he was attacked by paralysis. After many months in bed, he was able again to visit his garden, carried by Ju-man, a favourite monk. In 842 the poet Liu Yü-hsi, the last survivor of his intimate friends, and a constant visitor at the monastery, 'went to wander with Yüan Chên in Hades'. The monk Ju-man also died. The remaining years of Po's life were spent in collecting and arranging his complete works. He died in 846, leaving instructions that his funeral should be without pomp and that he should be buried by Ju-man's side in the Hsiang-shan monastery.

The most striking characteristic of Po Chü-i's poetry is its verbal simplicity. There is a story that he was in the habit of reading his poems to an old peasant woman, and altering any expression that she could not understand. Like Confucius, he regarded art solely as a means of conveying instruction. He accordingly valued his didactic poems far above his other work; but it is obvious that much of his best poetry conveys no moral whatever. He admits, indeed, that among his 'miscellaneous' stanzas many were inspired by some momentary sensation or passing event. 'A single laugh or a single sigh were rapidly translated into verse.'

The Emperor Ming Huang (A.D. 685–762) in his old age was so enamoured of Lady Yang Kuei-fei that he neglected his Empire until his vassals revolted, and his armies refused to take orders. Forced to flee the capital, he escaped towards Ssechʻuan with his lady and his officials; but even then his own bodyguard threatened that, unless he gave her up, they would desert him. Finally they seized and slew her, whereupon the soldiers once more pledged their loyalty to the dynasty.

36. Chʻêng-ming is the name of a palace at Chʻang-an.

41. Yüan Chên (A.D. 779–831) was a native of Honan Fu. When he was twenty-two years old he met Po Chü-i at Chʻang-an, and the two poets became intimate friends. But in 805 Yüan was banished to a petty post in a distant province for provocative behaviour towards a high official. Later on he was restored to Imperial favour and rose to the highest offices of the State. He died at the age of fifty-two as Governor of Wu-chʻang in Hupeh.

46. The Sung dynasty poet Ou-yang Hsiu (born A.D. 1007 at Lu-ling in Kiangsi Province) was brought up in poverty by his mother, who taught him to write with a reed. He graduated first on the list of candidates for the highest degree, and obtained employment in the capital; but his career as an official was a chequered one, owing to his courageous defence of what he believed to be right, regardless of personal interest. He was always ready to befriend rising talent; but, as a lover of the ancients, he used his influence as an Examiner to check the growing craze for eccentric writing and reasoning. Although a theoretical opponent of Buddhism, he maintained friendly relations with priests, and his gentle easy-going nature made him a very different Conservative Leader from Han Yü. He was fond of wine and company, and spoke of himself as 'the drunken Governor, an old man with white hair, bald at the top of his head'.

All through the winter and spring the worm lives underground. On the first night of summer it issues and, in the thrill of its second birth, begins to sing in a shrill, woman's voice. It sings all night, and then is silent again for ever.

52. The wind-bell is hung in prominent corners or along the eaves of old temples and pagodas. When it is shaken by the wind it tinkles. In old Chinese poetic diction it is called 'the iron horse'.

INDEX OF FIRST LINES